50 All-American Diner Cookbook

By: Kelly Johnson

Table of Contents

- Classic Cheeseburger
- Bacon, Egg, and Cheese Sandwich
- Chicken Fried Steak with Gravy
- Meatloaf with Mashed Potatoes
- Philly Cheesesteak Sandwich
- Onion Rings with Spicy Ketchup
- Grilled Cheese Sandwich with Tomato Soup
- French Toast with Maple Syrup
- Pancakes with Butter and Syrup
- BLT Sandwich
- Country-Fried Chicken with Biscuits
- Hot Dog with All the Toppings
- Diner-Style Club Sandwich
- Reuben Sandwich
- Chicken and Waffles
- Breakfast Burrito
- Classic Sloppy Joes
- Tuna Salad Sandwich
- Corned Beef Hash
- Grilled Chicken Caesar Salad
- Chili Cheese Fries
- New York-style Bagel with Lox and Cream Cheese
- Pork Chops with Applesauce
- Shrimp and Grits
- Diner-Style Meatball Sub
- Chicken Pot Pie
- Crab Cakes with Tartar Sauce
- Buffalo Wings with Blue Cheese Dip
- Fried Catfish with Hushpuppies
- Diner-Style Potato Salad
- Coney Island Chili Dog
- Macaroni and Cheese with Bacon
- Egg Salad Sandwich
- Fish and Chips
- Grilled Chicken Cobb Salad

- Biscuits and Gravy
- Fried Green Tomatoes
- Sweet Potato Fries with Marshmallow Dip
- Beef and Cheddar Melt
- Classic American Cobb Salad
- Philly Soft Pretzel with Mustard
- Sizzling Fajitas
- BBQ Ribs with Coleslaw
- Hot Roast Beef Sandwich with Gravy
- Southern Fried Chicken Sandwich
- Diner-Style Stuffed Bell Peppers
- Chocolate Cream Pie
- Apple Pie a la Mode
- Banana Cream Pie
- Milkshakes (Chocolate, Vanilla, or Strawberry)

Classic Cheeseburger

Ingredients

- 1 lb ground beef (80/20)
- Salt and pepper to taste
- 4 hamburger buns
- 4 slices cheddar cheese
- Lettuce, tomato, and pickles for topping
- Ketchup and mustard for serving

Instructions

1. Preheat your grill or skillet over medium-high heat.
2. Form the ground beef into 4 patties, making a slight indentation in the center of each. Season both sides with salt and pepper.
3. Cook the patties for 3-4 minutes per side, or until desired doneness. During the last minute of cooking, top each patty with a slice of cheese to melt.
4. Toast the hamburger buns lightly on the grill or skillet.
5. Assemble the burgers by placing the cooked patties on the buns and adding lettuce, tomato, pickles, and condiments. Serve immediately.

Bacon, Egg, and Cheese Sandwich

Ingredients

- 2 slices bread (your choice)
- 2 slices bacon
- 1 egg
- 1 slice cheddar cheese
- Butter for toasting
- Salt and pepper to taste

Instructions

1. Cook the bacon in a skillet over medium heat until crispy. Remove from the skillet and set aside.
2. In the same skillet, crack the egg and cook to your desired level (fried, scrambled, etc.). Season with salt and pepper.
3. Butter the bread and toast in a separate skillet until golden brown.
4. Assemble the sandwich by placing the cooked bacon, egg, and slice of cheese between the toasted bread slices. Serve immediately.

Chicken Fried Steak with Gravy

Ingredients

- 2 beef cube steaks
- 1 cup all-purpose flour
- 1 tsp salt
- 1/2 tsp black pepper
- 1/2 tsp garlic powder
- 1/4 tsp cayenne pepper
- 1 egg, beaten
- 1 cup buttermilk
- Vegetable oil for frying
- 1/2 cup chicken broth
- 1/2 cup milk
- 2 tbsp all-purpose flour (for gravy)
- Salt and pepper to taste

Instructions

1. In a shallow bowl, combine the flour, salt, pepper, garlic powder, and cayenne. In another bowl, whisk together the egg and buttermilk.
2. Dip each cube steak into the egg mixture, then coat in the flour mixture.
3. Heat oil in a skillet over medium-high heat. Fry the steaks for 3-4 minutes per side until golden and crispy. Remove and set aside.
4. For the gravy, use the same skillet and whisk in 2 tbsp of flour, cooking for 1-2 minutes. Gradually add chicken broth and milk, whisking until smooth. Simmer until thickened, then season with salt and pepper.
5. Serve the chicken-fried steak topped with gravy.

Meatloaf with Mashed Potatoes

Ingredients for Meatloaf

- 1 lb ground beef
- 1/2 cup breadcrumbs
- 1/4 cup milk
- 1/4 cup ketchup
- 1 egg, beaten
- 1 small onion, finely chopped
- 1 tsp salt
- 1/2 tsp black pepper

Ingredients for Mashed Potatoes

- 4 medium potatoes, peeled and cubed
- 1/2 cup milk
- 2 tbsp butter
- Salt and pepper to taste

Instructions

1. Preheat the oven to 375°F (190°C).
2. In a large bowl, mix together all the meatloaf ingredients until well combined. Shape into a loaf and place it on a baking sheet.
3. Bake for 50-60 minutes, or until cooked through. Optionally, top with extra ketchup in the last 10 minutes of baking.
4. For mashed potatoes, boil the cubed potatoes in salted water for 15-20 minutes until tender. Drain and mash with milk, butter, salt, and pepper.
5. Serve slices of meatloaf with mashed potatoes on the side.

Philly Cheesesteak Sandwich

Ingredients

- 1 lb thinly sliced ribeye steak
- 1 onion, sliced
- 1 green bell pepper, sliced
- 4 hoagie rolls
- 4 slices provolone cheese
- 2 tbsp olive oil
- Salt and pepper to taste

Instructions

1. Heat 1 tbsp olive oil in a skillet over medium heat. Add onions and peppers and cook until softened, about 5-7 minutes. Remove from the skillet and set aside.
2. In the same skillet, add the remaining oil and cook the sliced steak until browned, about 5-6 minutes. Season with salt and pepper.
3. Place the cooked onions and peppers back in the skillet with the steak.
4. Split the hoagie rolls and toast lightly.
5. Pile the steak and vegetable mixture onto the rolls and top with a slice of provolone cheese. Serve immediately.

Onion Rings with Spicy Ketchup

Ingredients

- 2 large onions, sliced into rings
- 1 cup buttermilk
- 1 cup all-purpose flour
- 1/2 tsp garlic powder
- 1/2 tsp paprika
- 1/4 tsp cayenne pepper
- Salt and pepper to taste
- Vegetable oil for frying
- 1/2 cup ketchup
- 1 tbsp sriracha sauce

Instructions

1. Soak the onion rings in buttermilk for at least 30 minutes.
2. In a bowl, mix the flour, garlic powder, paprika, cayenne, salt, and pepper.
3. Heat oil in a skillet over medium-high heat.
4. Dredge the soaked onion rings in the seasoned flour mixture and fry for 3-4 minutes until golden brown and crispy. Remove and drain on paper towels.
5. Mix ketchup and sriracha for a spicy dipping sauce. Serve the onion rings with the sauce.

Grilled Cheese Sandwich with Tomato Soup

Ingredients for Grilled Cheese

- 4 slices bread
- 4 slices cheddar cheese
- Butter for spreading

Ingredients for Tomato Soup

- 2 tbsp olive oil
- 1 onion, chopped
- 2 cloves garlic, minced
- 1 can (28 oz) crushed tomatoes
- 2 cups vegetable broth
- Salt and pepper to taste

Instructions

1. For the soup, heat olive oil in a pot over medium heat. Sauté onion and garlic until softened.
2. Add crushed tomatoes and vegetable broth. Bring to a simmer and cook for 20 minutes. Season with salt and pepper.
3. For the grilled cheese, butter the bread and place a slice of cheese between two slices of bread. Grill in a pan over medium heat until golden brown on both sides.
4. Serve the grilled cheese with a bowl of tomato soup.

French Toast with Maple Syrup

Ingredients

- 4 slices bread
- 2 eggs
- 1/2 cup milk
- 1 tsp vanilla extract
- 1/4 tsp cinnamon
- Butter for cooking
- Maple syrup for serving

Instructions

1. Whisk together eggs, milk, vanilla, and cinnamon in a bowl.
2. Heat butter in a skillet over medium heat.
3. Dip the bread into the egg mixture, coating both sides, and cook in the skillet for 2-3 minutes per side, until golden brown.
4. Serve the French toast with maple syrup.

Pancakes with Butter and Syrup

Ingredients

- 1 cup all-purpose flour
- 2 tbsp sugar
- 1 tsp baking powder
- 1/2 tsp baking soda
- 1/4 tsp salt
- 3/4 cup buttermilk
- 1 egg
- 2 tbsp melted butter
- Butter and maple syrup for serving

Instructions

1. In a bowl, whisk together the flour, sugar, baking powder, baking soda, and salt.
2. In another bowl, mix the buttermilk, egg, and melted butter.
3. Pour the wet ingredients into the dry ingredients and stir until just combined.
4. Heat a non-stick skillet or griddle over medium heat and lightly grease it with butter.
5. Pour 1/4 cup of batter onto the skillet for each pancake. Cook until bubbles form on the surface, then flip and cook until golden brown.
6. Serve the pancakes with butter and maple syrup.

BLT Sandwich

Ingredients

- 4 slices of bread
- 4 slices of bacon
- 1 tomato, sliced
- Lettuce leaves
- Mayonnaise
- Salt and pepper to taste

Instructions

1. Cook the bacon in a skillet over medium heat until crispy.
2. Toast the bread slices and spread mayonnaise on one side of each slice.
3. Layer the bacon, tomato slices, and lettuce on two slices of bread.
4. Season with salt and pepper. Top with the other slices of bread.
5. Slice and serve.

Country-Fried Chicken with Biscuits

Ingredients for Chicken

- 4 boneless, skinless chicken breasts
- 1 cup buttermilk
- 1 cup all-purpose flour
- 1 tsp paprika
- 1/2 tsp garlic powder
- Salt and pepper to taste
- Vegetable oil for frying

Ingredients for Biscuits

- 2 cups all-purpose flour
- 2 1/2 tsp baking powder
- 1/2 tsp salt
- 1/2 cup butter, cold and cubed
- 3/4 cup milk

Instructions

1. For the chicken, marinate the chicken breasts in buttermilk for at least 30 minutes.
2. In a shallow bowl, mix the flour, paprika, garlic powder, salt, and pepper.
3. Heat oil in a large skillet over medium-high heat.
4. Dredge the chicken in the flour mixture and fry until golden brown and cooked through, about 6-7 minutes per side.
5. For the biscuits, preheat the oven to 425°F (220°C).
6. In a bowl, combine the flour, baking powder, and salt. Cut in the butter until the mixture resembles coarse crumbs.
7. Stir in the milk until just combined. Drop spoonfuls of dough onto a baking sheet.
8. Bake for 12-15 minutes, until golden brown.
9. Serve the fried chicken with the biscuits.

Hot Dog with All the Toppings

Ingredients

- 4 hot dog buns
- 4 beef hot dogs
- Ketchup
- Mustard
- Relish
- Chopped onions
- Sauerkraut
- Shredded cheese (optional)

Instructions

1. Cook the hot dogs according to your preference: grill, boil, or pan-fry.
2. Toast the buns lightly on the grill or in the oven.
3. Place each hot dog in a bun and top with ketchup, mustard, relish, onions, and sauerkraut.
4. Add shredded cheese if desired. Serve immediately.

Diner-Style Club Sandwich

Ingredients

- 3 slices of bread (preferably toasted)
- 4 slices of turkey
- 4 slices of bacon
- Lettuce leaves
- Tomato slices
- Mayonnaise
- Salt and pepper to taste

Instructions

1. Spread mayonnaise on one side of each slice of bread.
2. On one slice of bread, layer turkey, bacon, lettuce, and tomato.
3. Top with the second slice of bread and repeat the layering.
4. Place the third slice of bread on top, and cut the sandwich into quarters.
5. Serve with chips or a side salad.

Reuben Sandwich

Ingredients

- 2 slices rye bread
- 4 oz corned beef
- 2 slices Swiss cheese
- 1/4 cup sauerkraut, drained
- 2 tbsp Russian dressing
- Butter for grilling

Instructions

1. Spread Russian dressing on one side of each slice of bread.
2. Layer the corned beef, Swiss cheese, and sauerkraut on one slice of bread.
3. Top with the second slice of bread, dressing side down.
4. Butter the outside of the sandwich and grill on medium heat until golden brown and the cheese is melted, about 3-4 minutes per side.
5. Serve hot.

Chicken and Waffles

Ingredients for Chicken

- 4 boneless chicken breasts
- 1 cup buttermilk
- 1 cup all-purpose flour
- 1 tsp paprika
- 1/2 tsp garlic powder
- Salt and pepper to taste
- Vegetable oil for frying

Ingredients for Waffles

- 2 cups all-purpose flour
- 2 tsp baking powder
- 1/2 tsp salt
- 2 eggs
- 1 3/4 cups milk
- 1/4 cup melted butter

Instructions

1. For the chicken, marinate the chicken breasts in buttermilk for at least 30 minutes.
2. In a shallow bowl, mix the flour, paprika, garlic powder, salt, and pepper.
3. Heat oil in a large skillet over medium-high heat.
4. Dredge the chicken in the flour mixture and fry until golden brown and cooked through, about 6-7 minutes per side.
5. For the waffles, preheat the waffle iron.
6. In a bowl, combine the flour, baking powder, and salt. In another bowl, whisk together the eggs, milk, and melted butter.
7. Add the wet ingredients to the dry ingredients and stir until just combined.
8. Pour the batter onto the waffle iron and cook according to the manufacturer's instructions.
9. Serve the fried chicken on top of the waffles, drizzle with syrup, and enjoy.

Breakfast Burrito

Ingredients

- 2 large eggs
- 1/4 cup milk
- 1/4 cup shredded cheese (cheddar or your preference)
- 1/4 cup cooked bacon or sausage, crumbled
- 1/4 cup diced bell peppers and onions
- 1/4 cup salsa
- 1 large flour tortilla
- Salt and pepper to taste

Instructions

1. Whisk the eggs, milk, salt, and pepper in a bowl.
2. Heat a non-stick skillet over medium heat and scramble the eggs until cooked through.
3. Warm the tortilla in a separate skillet or microwave for a few seconds.
4. Add the scrambled eggs, cheese, bacon or sausage, bell peppers, onions, and salsa to the center of the tortilla.
5. Fold the sides of the tortilla and roll it up to form the burrito.
6. Serve warm.

Classic Sloppy Joes

Ingredients

- 1 lb ground beef
- 1/2 onion, chopped
- 1/2 bell pepper, chopped
- 1 can (8 oz) tomato sauce
- 2 tbsp ketchup
- 1 tbsp mustard
- 1 tbsp Worcestershire sauce
- 1/4 cup brown sugar
- Salt and pepper to taste
- 4 hamburger buns

Instructions

1. In a skillet, cook the ground beef over medium heat until browned, breaking it apart as it cooks.
2. Add the chopped onion and bell pepper and cook until softened, about 5 minutes.
3. Stir in the tomato sauce, ketchup, mustard, Worcestershire sauce, and brown sugar.
4. Let it simmer on low heat for about 15 minutes, stirring occasionally.
5. Season with salt and pepper to taste.
6. Spoon the mixture onto hamburger buns and serve.

Tuna Salad Sandwich

Ingredients

- 1 can tuna, drained
- 1/4 cup mayonnaise
- 1 tbsp Dijon mustard
- 1/2 tbsp lemon juice
- 1/4 cup chopped celery
- 1/4 cup chopped red onion
- Salt and pepper to taste
- 2 slices bread (whole wheat, white, or your choice)

Instructions

1. In a bowl, combine the tuna, mayonnaise, Dijon mustard, and lemon juice.
2. Add the chopped celery and red onion, and mix until well combined.
3. Season with salt and pepper to taste.
4. Spread the tuna salad onto a slice of bread and top with the other slice.
5. Serve immediately, or refrigerate until ready to eat.

Corned Beef Hash

Ingredients

- 2 cups cooked corned beef, chopped
- 2 large potatoes, peeled and diced
- 1/2 onion, chopped
- 2 tbsp olive oil
- 2 tbsp butter
- Salt and pepper to taste
- 2 eggs (optional, for topping)

Instructions

1. Boil the diced potatoes in salted water until tender, about 10 minutes. Drain well.
2. Heat olive oil and butter in a skillet over medium heat. Add the chopped onion and cook until softened.
3. Add the cooked potatoes to the skillet and fry until they begin to crisp up, about 5-7 minutes.
4. Add the chopped corned beef and continue to cook for another 5 minutes until everything is well browned.
5. Season with salt and pepper to taste.
6. Optionally, top with fried or poached eggs and serve.

Grilled Chicken Caesar Salad

Ingredients

- 2 boneless, skinless chicken breasts
- 1 tbsp olive oil
- Salt and pepper to taste
- 4 cups romaine lettuce, chopped
- 1/2 cup Caesar dressing
- 1/4 cup grated Parmesan cheese
- Croutons for topping

Instructions

1. Preheat the grill or grill pan to medium-high heat.
2. Rub the chicken breasts with olive oil and season with salt and pepper.
3. Grill the chicken for 6-7 minutes per side, or until cooked through. Let it rest for a few minutes, then slice.
4. Toss the chopped lettuce with Caesar dressing.
5. Top the salad with the grilled chicken, grated Parmesan, and croutons.
6. Serve immediately.

Chili Cheese Fries

Ingredients

- 1 lb frozen French fries
- 1 can (15 oz) chili (or homemade chili)
- 1 cup shredded cheddar cheese
- Sour cream (optional)
- Chopped green onions (optional)

Instructions

1. Bake the French fries according to the package directions.
2. While the fries are baking, heat the chili in a saucepan over medium heat.
3. Once the fries are crispy and golden, remove them from the oven and place them on a serving dish.
4. Pour the heated chili over the fries and top with shredded cheddar cheese.
5. Place the fries back in the oven for a few minutes until the cheese melts.
6. Optionally, garnish with sour cream and chopped green onions before serving.

New York-style Bagel with Lox and Cream Cheese

Ingredients

- 2 bagels, sliced in half
- 4 oz cream cheese
- 4 oz smoked salmon (lox)
- 1/4 red onion, thinly sliced
- Capers (optional)
- Fresh dill (optional)

Instructions

1. Toast the bagel halves to your desired level of crispness.
2. Spread cream cheese generously on each half.
3. Layer the smoked salmon on top of the cream cheese.
4. Top with thinly sliced red onions and capers, if using.
5. Garnish with fresh dill and serve.

Pork Chops with Applesauce

Ingredients

- 4 bone-in pork chops
- 2 tbsp olive oil
- Salt and pepper to taste
- 1/2 tsp cinnamon
- 1/4 tsp nutmeg
- 2 cups applesauce (store-bought or homemade)

Instructions

1. Heat the olive oil in a skillet over medium-high heat.
2. Season the pork chops with salt, pepper, cinnamon, and nutmeg.
3. Sear the pork chops in the skillet for 4-5 minutes per side, until golden brown and cooked through.
4. While the pork chops are cooking, heat the applesauce in a separate saucepan over low heat.
5. Serve the pork chops with a spoonful of warm applesauce on the side.

Shrimp and Grits

Ingredients

- 1 lb shrimp, peeled and deveined
- 1 cup grits
- 2 cups water
- 1 tbsp butter
- 1 tbsp olive oil
- 1/2 onion, chopped
- 2 cloves garlic, minced
- 1/2 cup heavy cream
- 1/2 cup shredded cheddar cheese
- Salt and pepper to taste
- 1 tbsp lemon juice
- Chopped green onions for garnish

Instructions

1. In a pot, bring the water to a boil. Stir in the grits, reduce heat, and cook until thickened, about 5-7 minutes.
2. Stir in butter, heavy cream, and cheddar cheese. Season with salt and pepper.
3. In a skillet, heat olive oil over medium heat. Add the onion and garlic, cooking until softened.
4. Add the shrimp to the skillet and cook for 2-3 minutes per side until pink and cooked through.
5. Stir in lemon juice and adjust seasoning.
6. Serve the shrimp over the creamy grits, garnished with chopped green onions.

Diner-Style Meatball Sub

Ingredients

- 1 lb ground beef
- 1/4 cup breadcrumbs
- 1/4 cup grated Parmesan cheese
- 1 egg
- 1/4 cup milk
- 2 cloves garlic, minced
- 1/2 cup marinara sauce
- 4 sub rolls
- 1 cup mozzarella cheese, shredded
- Salt and pepper to taste

Instructions

1. Preheat the oven to 375°F (190°C).
2. In a bowl, combine the ground beef, breadcrumbs, Parmesan, egg, milk, garlic, salt, and pepper. Form into 8-10 meatballs.
3. Place meatballs on a baking sheet and bake for 20-25 minutes, until browned and cooked through.
4. Heat marinara sauce in a saucepan and add the meatballs, simmering for 5 minutes.
5. Slice the sub rolls and spoon meatballs and sauce onto the rolls. Top with shredded mozzarella.
6. Place the subs under the broiler for 2-3 minutes until the cheese melts.
7. Serve hot.

Chicken Pot Pie

Ingredients

- 2 cups cooked chicken, shredded
- 1 cup frozen peas and carrots
- 1/3 cup butter
- 1/3 cup flour
- 2 cups chicken broth
- 1 cup milk
- Salt and pepper to taste
- 1/2 tsp thyme
- 1/2 tsp garlic powder
- 1 package pie crusts (or homemade if preferred)

Instructions

1. Preheat the oven to 375°F (190°C).
2. In a large skillet, melt the butter over medium heat. Stir in the flour and cook for 1 minute.
3. Gradually whisk in the chicken broth and milk, stirring until thickened.
4. Add the shredded chicken, peas, carrots, salt, pepper, thyme, and garlic powder. Stir to combine.
5. Roll out the pie crusts and fit one into a pie dish. Pour the chicken mixture into the crust.
6. Top with the second pie crust, sealing the edges. Cut slits in the top to allow steam to escape.
7. Bake for 30-35 minutes until the crust is golden brown.
8. Serve warm.

Crab Cakes with Tartar Sauce

Ingredients

- 1 lb lump crab meat
- 1/2 cup breadcrumbs
- 1 egg
- 1/4 cup mayonnaise
- 1 tbsp Dijon mustard
- 1 tbsp lemon juice
- 1 tsp Old Bay seasoning
- Salt and pepper to taste
- 2 tbsp butter
- For tartar sauce: 1/2 cup mayonnaise, 2 tbsp chopped pickles, 1 tsp lemon juice, salt to taste

Instructions

1. In a bowl, mix together the crab meat, breadcrumbs, egg, mayonnaise, mustard, lemon juice, Old Bay seasoning, salt, and pepper.
2. Form the mixture into 4-6 cakes.
3. In a skillet, melt the butter over medium heat. Cook the crab cakes for 3-4 minutes per side until golden brown.
4. For the tartar sauce, combine mayonnaise, chopped pickles, lemon juice, and salt in a bowl.
5. Serve the crab cakes with the tartar sauce on the side.

Buffalo Wings with Blue Cheese Dip

Ingredients

- 1 lb chicken wings
- 1/2 cup buffalo sauce
- 2 tbsp melted butter
- 1/2 cup blue cheese dressing
- 1 tbsp sour cream
- 1 tbsp lemon juice
- Chopped celery and carrots for garnish

Instructions

1. Preheat the oven to 400°F (200°C).
2. Arrange the chicken wings on a baking sheet and bake for 25-30 minutes, flipping halfway through, until crispy.
3. In a bowl, mix the buffalo sauce and melted butter.
4. Toss the cooked wings in the buffalo sauce mixture until well coated.
5. For the dip, mix blue cheese dressing, sour cream, and lemon juice in a bowl.
6. Serve the wings with the blue cheese dip and garnish with celery and carrots.

Fried Catfish with Hushpuppies

Ingredients

- 4 catfish fillets
- 1 cup cornmeal
- 1/2 cup flour
- 1 tbsp paprika
- Salt and pepper to taste
- 1 egg
- 1/2 cup buttermilk
- Oil for frying

For Hushpuppies:

- 1 cup cornmeal
- 1/4 cup flour
- 1 tsp baking powder
- 1/4 cup diced onion
- 1 egg
- 1/2 cup buttermilk
- Salt and pepper to taste

Instructions

1. For the hushpuppies, combine cornmeal, flour, baking powder, onion, egg, buttermilk, salt, and pepper in a bowl. Mix well.
2. Heat oil in a deep fryer or large skillet to 350°F (175°C).
3. Drop spoonfuls of hushpuppy batter into the hot oil and fry until golden brown, about 3-4 minutes.
4. For the catfish, whisk together cornmeal, flour, paprika, salt, and pepper.
5. Dip each catfish fillet in buttermilk, then coat in the cornmeal mixture.
6. Fry the fillets in the hot oil for 5-6 minutes per side, until crispy and golden.
7. Serve the catfish with hushpuppies and your favorite dipping sauce.

Diner-Style Potato Salad

Ingredients

- 4 large potatoes, peeled and diced
- 1/2 cup mayonnaise
- 2 tbsp Dijon mustard
- 1 tbsp vinegar
- 1/4 cup diced pickles
- 1/4 cup diced celery
- 1/4 cup diced red onion
- Salt and pepper to taste
- Chopped parsley for garnish

Instructions

1. Boil the diced potatoes in salted water until tender, about 10 minutes. Drain and let cool.
2. In a large bowl, combine the mayonnaise, mustard, vinegar, pickles, celery, and red onion.
3. Add the cooled potatoes to the dressing mixture and stir to coat.
4. Season with salt and pepper.
5. Garnish with chopped parsley and refrigerate for at least an hour before serving.

Coney Island Chili Dog

Ingredients

- 4 hot dog buns
- 4 beef hot dogs
- 1 can chili (or homemade chili)
- 1/2 cup diced onions
- 1/2 cup shredded cheddar cheese
- Mustard and ketchup for topping (optional)

Instructions

1. Heat the chili in a saucepan over low heat.
2. Grill or boil the hot dogs until cooked through.
3. Toast the hot dog buns on a grill or in a toaster.
4. Place the cooked hot dogs in the buns and top with warm chili.
5. Sprinkle with diced onions and shredded cheddar cheese.
6. Optionally, add mustard and ketchup before serving.

Macaroni and Cheese with Bacon

Ingredients

- 2 cups elbow macaroni
- 4 slices bacon, chopped
- 2 cups shredded cheddar cheese
- 1 cup milk
- 2 tbsp butter
- 2 tbsp flour
- 1/2 tsp garlic powder
- Salt and pepper to taste
- 1/4 cup bread crumbs (optional)

Instructions

1. Cook the macaroni according to package instructions, drain, and set aside.
2. In a large skillet, cook the chopped bacon until crispy. Remove and set aside.
3. In the same skillet, melt butter and whisk in flour to form a roux. Cook for 1-2 minutes.
4. Gradually whisk in milk and cook until the sauce thickens.
5. Stir in shredded cheddar cheese until melted and smooth. Season with garlic powder, salt, and pepper.
6. Add the cooked macaroni and bacon to the cheese sauce, stirring to combine.
7. Top with breadcrumbs if desired and bake in a 375°F (190°C) oven for 10-15 minutes until golden and bubbly.
8. Serve hot.

Egg Salad Sandwich

Ingredients

- 6 boiled eggs, peeled and chopped
- 1/4 cup mayonnaise
- 1 tbsp Dijon mustard
- 1 tbsp fresh parsley, chopped
- Salt and pepper to taste
- 4 slices bread (or more if making multiple sandwiches)

Instructions

1. In a bowl, mix together chopped boiled eggs, mayonnaise, mustard, parsley, salt, and pepper.
2. Spread the egg salad on a slice of bread.
3. Top with another slice of bread to form a sandwich.
4. Serve with a side of chips or pickle.

Fish and Chips

Ingredients

- 4 pieces white fish fillets (cod or haddock)
- 1 cup flour
- 1/2 cup corn starch
- 1 tsp baking powder
- 1 tsp salt
- 1 cup sparkling water
- Oil for frying
- 4 large potatoes, cut into fries
- Salt to taste

Instructions

1. Preheat the oil for frying to 350°F (175°C).
2. Mix flour, corn starch, baking powder, and salt in a bowl. Gradually whisk in sparkling water to form a smooth batter.
3. Coat the fish fillets in the batter and fry in the hot oil until golden brown and crispy, about 5-6 minutes.
4. While the fish is cooking, fry the potato fries in the same oil until crispy and golden, about 4-5 minutes.
5. Drain both the fish and fries on paper towels, and season with salt.
6. Serve the fish and chips with malt vinegar or tartar sauce.

Grilled Chicken Cobb Salad

Ingredients

- 2 boneless, skinless chicken breasts
- 1 tbsp olive oil
- 1 tsp paprika
- Salt and pepper to taste
- 4 cups mixed salad greens
- 1/2 cup cherry tomatoes, halved
- 1/4 cup red onion, thinly sliced
- 1/4 cup blue cheese crumbles
- 2 hard-boiled eggs, sliced
- 1 avocado, sliced
- 4 slices bacon, cooked and crumbled
- 1/4 cup ranch dressing (or dressing of choice)

Instructions

1. Preheat the grill to medium heat.
2. Rub the chicken breasts with olive oil, paprika, salt, and pepper. Grill for 6-7 minutes per side until fully cooked.
3. Slice the chicken into strips.
4. In a large bowl, toss the salad greens, cherry tomatoes, red onion, blue cheese, eggs, avocado, and bacon.
5. Top the salad with the grilled chicken and drizzle with your choice of dressing.
6. Serve immediately.

Biscuits and Gravy

Ingredients

- 1 can of refrigerated biscuits
- 1 lb breakfast sausage
- 1/4 cup flour
- 2 cups milk
- Salt and pepper to taste

Instructions

1. Preheat the oven and bake the biscuits according to package instructions.
2. While the biscuits are baking, cook the sausage in a skillet over medium heat, breaking it up into crumbles.
3. Once the sausage is cooked, sprinkle flour over the sausage and cook for 1-2 minutes.
4. Gradually whisk in milk and cook until the gravy thickens, about 5 minutes.
5. Season with salt and pepper to taste.
6. Split the biscuits in half and top with the sausage gravy.
7. Serve hot.

Fried Green Tomatoes

Ingredients

- 4 green tomatoes, sliced
- 1 cup cornmeal
- 1/2 cup flour
- 1 tsp salt
- 1/2 tsp black pepper
- 1/2 tsp cayenne pepper (optional)
- 1 egg, beaten
- Oil for frying

Instructions

1. Heat oil in a skillet over medium-high heat.
2. In a bowl, mix together cornmeal, flour, salt, pepper, and cayenne.
3. Dip each tomato slice in the beaten egg, then dredge in the cornmeal mixture.
4. Fry the coated tomato slices in the hot oil for 2-3 minutes per side until crispy and golden brown.
5. Drain on paper towels and serve hot.

Sweet Potato Fries with Marshmallow Dip

Ingredients

- 2 large sweet potatoes, peeled and cut into fries
- 2 tbsp olive oil
- 1/2 tsp paprika
- Salt to taste
- 1/2 cup marshmallow fluff
- 1/4 cup sour cream
- 1 tbsp honey

Instructions

1. Preheat the oven to 400°F (200°C).
2. Toss the sweet potato fries with olive oil, paprika, and salt.
3. Spread the fries in a single layer on a baking sheet and bake for 25-30 minutes, flipping halfway through.
4. In a small bowl, mix together marshmallow fluff, sour cream, and honey to make the dip.
5. Serve the fries hot with the marshmallow dip on the side.

Beef and Cheddar Melt

Ingredients

- 1 lb roast beef, thinly sliced
- 4 slices cheddar cheese
- 4 hoagie rolls
- 1/4 cup mayonnaise
- 1 tbsp Dijon mustard
- 1 tbsp horseradish sauce (optional)
- 1 tbsp butter

Instructions

1. Preheat the oven to 350°F (175°C).
2. In a bowl, mix together mayonnaise, Dijon mustard, and horseradish sauce (if using).
3. Spread the mayonnaise mixture on the inside of the hoagie rolls.
4. Layer the sliced roast beef and cheddar cheese in the rolls.
5. Butter the outside of the rolls and place them on a baking sheet.
6. Bake for 10-12 minutes, until the cheese is melted and the rolls are crispy.
7. Serve warm.

Classic American Cobb Salad

Ingredients

- 2 boneless, skinless chicken breasts
- 4 cups mixed greens
- 2 hard-boiled eggs, chopped
- 1 avocado, sliced
- 1/2 cup cherry tomatoes, halved
- 1/4 cup red onion, thinly sliced
- 1/4 cup blue cheese, crumbled
- 1/4 cup bacon, cooked and crumbled
- 1/4 cup dressing of choice (ranch, blue cheese, or vinaigrette)
- Salt and pepper to taste

Instructions

1. Grill or cook the chicken breasts, then slice them into strips.
2. In a large salad bowl, combine the mixed greens, hard-boiled eggs, avocado, cherry tomatoes, red onion, blue cheese, and bacon.
3. Add the sliced chicken on top and season with salt and pepper.
4. Drizzle with your choice of dressing.
5. Toss gently and serve.

Philly Soft Pretzel with Mustard

Ingredients

- 2 cups warm water
- 1 tbsp sugar
- 2 1/4 tsp active dry yeast
- 4 cups all-purpose flour
- 1 tsp salt
- 2 tbsp melted butter
- 1/4 cup baking soda
- Coarse salt for sprinkling
- Yellow mustard for serving

Instructions

1. In a bowl, combine warm water, sugar, and yeast. Let sit for 5 minutes to activate the yeast.
2. Add flour, salt, and melted butter to the yeast mixture, mixing until a dough forms. Knead the dough for about 5 minutes.
3. Cover and let rise for about 1 hour or until doubled in size.
4. Preheat the oven to 450°F (230°C).
5. Bring a pot of water to a boil and add baking soda.
6. Divide the dough into 8 portions and shape each into a pretzel.
7. Carefully drop each pretzel into the boiling water for about 30 seconds, then remove and place on a baking sheet.
8. Sprinkle with coarse salt and bake for 12-15 minutes until golden brown.
9. Serve with yellow mustard.

Sizzling Fajitas

Ingredients

- 1 lb chicken or beef (flank steak or chicken breasts), sliced thin
- 1 tbsp olive oil
- 1 onion, sliced
- 1 bell pepper, sliced
- 1 tsp chili powder
- 1 tsp cumin
- 1/2 tsp paprika
- Salt and pepper to taste
- 1 tbsp lime juice
- 8 small flour tortillas
- Sour cream, guacamole, salsa, and cilantro for garnish

Instructions

1. In a large skillet or cast-iron pan, heat olive oil over medium-high heat.
2. Add sliced chicken or beef and cook until browned and cooked through.
3. Add the sliced onion and bell pepper, and cook until soft, about 5-7 minutes.
4. Stir in chili powder, cumin, paprika, salt, and pepper. Cook for another 2-3 minutes.
5. Add lime juice and remove from heat.
6. Warm the tortillas in a separate pan or microwave.
7. Serve the fajita mixture on the sizzling skillet with tortillas on the side. Top with sour cream, guacamole, salsa, and cilantro.

BBQ Ribs with Coleslaw

Ingredients

- 2 racks of baby back ribs
- 1/2 cup BBQ sauce (store-bought or homemade)
- 1 tbsp brown sugar
- 1 tsp paprika
- 1/2 tsp garlic powder
- 1/2 tsp onion powder
- Salt and pepper to taste
- 2 cups shredded cabbage
- 1 carrot, grated
- 1/2 cup mayonnaise
- 1 tbsp apple cider vinegar
- 1 tsp Dijon mustard
- 1 tbsp sugar

Instructions

1. Preheat the oven to 300°F (150°C).
2. Mix the brown sugar, paprika, garlic powder, onion powder, salt, and pepper in a bowl. Rub the seasoning mixture over the ribs.
3. Wrap the ribs in foil and bake for 2.5 to 3 hours until tender.
4. During the last 30 minutes, brush the ribs with BBQ sauce and bake uncovered for the final touch.
5. For the coleslaw, combine shredded cabbage, grated carrot, mayonnaise, apple cider vinegar, Dijon mustard, and sugar in a bowl. Mix until combined.
6. Serve the BBQ ribs with a side of coleslaw.

Hot Roast Beef Sandwich with Gravy

Ingredients

- 1 lb roast beef, thinly sliced
- 4 slices of bread (preferably French or a hearty roll)
- 1 cup beef broth
- 2 tbsp flour
- 2 tbsp butter
- Salt and pepper to taste
- 1/2 tsp garlic powder
- 1/2 tsp onion powder

Instructions

1. In a skillet, melt butter over medium heat.
2. Add flour and whisk to create a roux. Cook for 1-2 minutes.
3. Slowly add beef broth while continuing to whisk until the gravy thickens, about 5 minutes.
4. Season with salt, pepper, garlic powder, and onion powder.
5. Toast the bread slices and layer with slices of roast beef.
6. Pour the gravy over the sandwich and serve hot.

Southern Fried Chicken Sandwich

Ingredients

- 2 chicken breasts, boneless and skinless
- 1 cup buttermilk
- 1 cup all-purpose flour
- 1 tsp paprika
- 1 tsp garlic powder
- 1 tsp onion powder
- 1/2 tsp cayenne pepper
- Salt and pepper to taste
- 4 sandwich buns
- Pickles, lettuce, and tomatoes for garnish
- Vegetable oil for frying

Instructions

1. In a bowl, soak the chicken breasts in buttermilk for at least 1 hour or overnight in the fridge.
2. In a separate shallow dish, combine flour, paprika, garlic powder, onion powder, cayenne, salt, and pepper.
3. Heat oil in a large pan over medium-high heat.
4. Dredge the chicken breasts in the flour mixture, pressing to coat.
5. Fry the chicken for 4-6 minutes per side, or until golden brown and cooked through.
6. Toast the sandwich buns and assemble with fried chicken, pickles, lettuce, and tomatoes. Serve immediately.

Diner-Style Stuffed Bell Peppers

Ingredients

- 4 bell peppers, tops cut off and seeds removed
- 1 lb ground beef
- 1/2 cup onion, chopped
- 1 cup cooked rice
- 1 can (14 oz) diced tomatoes
- 1/2 tsp garlic powder
- 1/2 tsp dried oregano
- Salt and pepper to taste
- 1 cup shredded cheddar cheese

Instructions

1. Preheat the oven to 375°F (190°C).
2. In a skillet, cook ground beef and onion over medium heat until browned. Drain excess fat.
3. Add cooked rice, diced tomatoes, garlic powder, oregano, salt, and pepper to the beef mixture. Stir to combine.
4. Stuff the bell peppers with the beef and rice mixture. Place the stuffed peppers in a baking dish.
5. Top with shredded cheddar cheese and cover with foil.
6. Bake for 25-30 minutes, then remove foil and bake for an additional 10 minutes until the peppers are tender and cheese is melted.

Chocolate Cream Pie

Ingredients

- 1 pre-baked pie crust
- 1 1/2 cups whole milk
- 1/2 cup heavy cream
- 3/4 cup sugar
- 1/4 cup cornstarch
- 1/2 tsp salt
- 3/4 cup semi-sweet chocolate chips
- 4 large egg yolks
- 2 tbsp butter
- 1 tsp vanilla extract
- Whipped cream for topping

Instructions

1. In a medium saucepan, combine milk, heavy cream, sugar, cornstarch, and salt. Cook over medium heat, whisking constantly until thickened, about 5 minutes.
2. Remove from heat and stir in chocolate chips until melted.
3. In a separate bowl, whisk egg yolks. Slowly pour a small amount of the hot mixture into the yolks to temper them, then add the egg yolk mixture back into the saucepan.
4. Cook the mixture for another 2 minutes, then remove from heat. Stir in butter and vanilla.
5. Pour the chocolate filling into the pie crust and smooth the top.
6. Refrigerate for at least 4 hours. Top with whipped cream before serving.

Apple Pie a la Mode

Ingredients

- 1 pre-baked pie crust
- 6 cups apples (such as Granny Smith), peeled and sliced
- 3/4 cup sugar
- 1/4 cup brown sugar
- 1 tsp cinnamon
- 1/2 tsp nutmeg
- 1 tbsp lemon juice
- 2 tbsp butter
- Vanilla ice cream for serving

Instructions

1. Preheat the oven to 425°F (220°C).
2. In a bowl, combine apples, sugar, brown sugar, cinnamon, nutmeg, and lemon juice. Mix until apples are coated.
3. Pour the apple mixture into the pie crust. Dot with butter.
4. Cover with the second pie crust, crimping the edges to seal. Cut small slits in the top to allow steam to escape.
5. Bake for 45-50 minutes or until the crust is golden brown.
6. Let the pie cool slightly, then serve with a scoop of vanilla ice cream.

Banana Cream Pie

Ingredients

- 1 pre-baked pie crust
- 3 ripe bananas, sliced
- 2 cups whole milk
- 3/4 cup sugar
- 1/4 cup cornstarch
- 1/4 tsp salt
- 4 large egg yolks
- 2 tbsp butter
- 1 tsp vanilla extract
- Whipped cream for topping

Instructions

1. In a medium saucepan, combine milk, sugar, cornstarch, and salt. Cook over medium heat, whisking constantly until thickened, about 5 minutes.
2. Remove from heat and slowly add a small amount of the hot mixture into the egg yolks to temper them, then add the yolk mixture back into the saucepan.
3. Cook for another 2 minutes, then remove from heat. Stir in butter and vanilla extract.
4. Arrange the sliced bananas in the bottom of the pie crust. Pour the custard filling over the bananas.
5. Refrigerate for at least 4 hours. Top with whipped cream before serving.

Milkshakes (Chocolate, Vanilla, or Strawberry)

Ingredients

- 2 cups vanilla ice cream
- 1 cup milk
- 1/4 cup chocolate syrup (for chocolate milkshake)
- 1/4 cup fresh strawberries, mashed (for strawberry milkshake)
- 1 tsp vanilla extract (for vanilla milkshake)
- Whipped cream for topping

Instructions

1. In a blender, combine ice cream and milk.
2. For chocolate milkshake: Add chocolate syrup and blend until smooth.
3. For strawberry milkshake: Add mashed strawberries and blend until smooth.
4. For vanilla milkshake: Add vanilla extract and blend until smooth.
5. Pour into glasses and top with whipped cream before serving.

www.ingramcontent.com/pod-product-compliance
Lightning Source LLC
LaVergne TN
LVHW081330060526
838201LV00055B/2559